ZERO BUDGET MARKETING

USING PR TO YOUR ADVANTAGE

ASHISH GUPTA

Copyright © Ashish Gupta
All Rights Reserved.

ISBN 978-1-68494-467-5

This book has been published with all efforts taken to make the material error-free after the consent of the author. However, the author and the publisher do not assume and hereby disclaim any liability to any party for any loss, damage, or disruption caused by errors or omissions, whether such errors or omissions result from negligence, accident, or any other cause.

While every effort has been made to avoid any mistake or omission, this publication is being sold on the condition and understanding that neither the author nor the publishers or printers would be liable in any manner to any person by reason of any mistake or omission in this publication or for any action taken or omitted to be taken or advice rendered or accepted on the basis of this work. For any defect in printing or binding the publishers will be liable only to replace the defective copy by another copy of this work then available.

Contents

1. Introduction — 1
2. What Is Not Pr — 6
3. Who Should Have A Pr Strategy — 10
4. Write A Press Release — 16
5. Why Pr — 18
6. How Pr & Advertising Go Together — 21
7. Creating A Pr Strategy — 24
8. Step 1 - Identify Target Audience — 26
9. Step 2 - Creating A Plan For Each Audience — 29
10. Step 3 - Contact Management — 36
11. Step 4 - Writing Pr Communication — 42
12. Tools For Pr — 48
13. Conclusion — 49

CHAPTER ONE

INTRODUCTION

Before we begin our discussion on Public Relation (PR), we want you to leave aside any marketing budget you have. We will understand and explore the world of 'Public Relations' which is done on a zero budget. Yes, you read it right. Zero budget. You do not need a single penny to market your product using PR.

Till date, Tesla has not spent a single dollar on paid ads. Yet, we know how strong their marketing is. The method they use is 'Public Relations'. XIAOMI came to India a few years back and in no time went on to stand amongst the top 3 mobile sellers in the country, all this on a zero ad budget. The way they did it – 'Public Relations'.

In fact, you would be surprised to see how much can be achieved by PR. At times, PR, has the ability to beat advertising and that too with almost zero budget. Advertising will suck millions out of your marketing budget and still underperform PR.

However, sometimes PR may not get you the desired results. Thus, Public Relations and Advertisements both have their respective roles to play. For now, know that PR is at least equally powerful if not more, as advertising.

Think about politics. Think about the 'Modi Wave in 2014 elections'. What was it? Nothing but a large PR effort. No other form off advertising could have achieved what that PR campaign did. Thus, for small businesses PR is one of the most essential and underutilized aspects of marketing.

Lorose

HOW PEOPLE SEE YOU

Let us come back and focus on what Public Relation is. Most small business owners either do not understand the term itself or even if they do, they end up believing that it is only for the big and powerful. Let us first see what is PR and then check if it is only for the big. So, what is Public Relation? Public Relations Society of America defines it as – "Public Relation is a strategic communication process that builds mutually beneficial relationships between organizations and their public.

In simple terms, Public Relations means 'How People See You?' Those included in these 'people' are a very broad set. We will see that in a while. But for now, remember that 'how people see you' will determine 'how they treat you.' You can only expect to get the desired results if various stakeholders respect you and your work. This is where PR comes into the picture.

For instance, what investors think about you and your attitude towards their money will determine the ease while you raise the required funding amount. If investors look up to you as someone who respects investor interests, then you will be able to raise money at a cheaper cost i.e. for a lower interest rate or for a lower equity dilution.

How employees think about you will determine the company's employee retention ratio. If you have a very high employee relation, then you can attract the top talent and for compensation that is relatively lower than the market average. They would want to work with you.

Similarly, the way customers think about you will determine whether they buy from you or not. If they think highly of you, they will trust you. Else, growth and getting new customer business would become a challenge for you.

In other words, PR is a systematic effort to send updates to different stakeholders so that you can shape and influence what they think about you. Know that you cannot control what someone thinks about your business. But, you can definitely control what they know about you. This is within your control and this is where PR efforts are required.

> *PR people are storytellers. They create narratives to advance their agenda. PR can be used to protect, enhance or build reputations through the media, social media, or self-produced communications. A good PR*

practitioner will analyze the organization, find the positive messages and translate those messages into positive stories. When the news is bad, they can formulate the best response and mitigate the damage.

Forbes

Public relations specialist is an image shaper. Their job is to generate positive publicity for their client and enhance their reputation... They keep the public informed about the activity of government agencies, explain policy, and manage political campaigns. Public relations people working for a company may handle consumer relations, or the relationship between parts of the company such as the managers and employees, or different branch offices."

The Princeton Review

> **STORIES**
>
> # Starting from a small room, this entrepreneur built a Rs 1,000 Cr snacks company
>
> Prataap Snacks is a large-scale snacks manufacturer that runs nine manufacturing facilities, and has an extensive distribution network of 240 super-stockists and more than 4,100 distributors.
>
> By Rishabh Mansur

YOURSTORY

Imagine the kind of impact such an article will make in your business if it appears in a national major newspaper. Think about how this will add creditability to your business. This article was published by YourStory, a news site with an average monthly viewership of 12 million. Imagine the creditability it gives to the company.

CHAPTER TWO

WHAT IS NOT PR

Public Relations efforts are very different from other marketing efforts. Particularly, PR is sometimes a substitute for advertising. This is also a reason why PR is often confused with advertising. Let us clearly understand the difference between PR and advertisement. Below are the major differences between the two. These will also explain to you the various features of Public Relations.

PAID VS EARNED

Advertising is a paid medium of marketing. In advertising, you create an ad and pay a media house for the ad space. That can be in newspapers, TV, radio, outdoor banners, digital ads, etc. Wherever you are required to pay to be covered is a form of advertising. At the same time, PR coverage is earned for your work. Only if the quality of your work is very high, or you are doing something new and different, media houses would like to cover you.

Here you do not have to pay anything to media houses. They cover your story because they think that your story will interest their target audience. In this way, they create an outside narrative for you. Repeated media coverage builds a narrative for your company

BUILDS EXPOSURE VS BUILDS TRUST

Advertisement is in your control. You control what you write and how large will your reach be based on your budget. So, the primary role of advertisement is to build exposure. Get your offer to as many people as possible, even if you are starting in a dorm room with no background. At the same time, PR builds trust. Because your story would be covered by a third party such as Times of India or YourStory, you do not decide the content of the coverage, the media house does.

So, whenever a reader comes across this piece in a newspaper or magazine, he would trust you more because a credible third party has written the piece. We already saw earlier that if you do not build trust, it would be very difficult for you to sell. PR does that for you. So, you must build trust using PR and then get exposure through advertisements.

SKEPTICAL AUDIENCE VS THIRD-PARTY VALIDATION

Adding on to our earlier discussion, in an ad, we can control all that we want to say. However, that is not the case in PR. Even if the Times of India decides to write an article about you, you have no say over what exactly will they write. At times, they may write negatively as well. Thus, whenever a person sees an ad, he becomes skeptical and questions whether it is true or not. However, if he reads an article in a newspaper or magazine, he instantly trusts it because of third-party validation.

GUARANTEED PLACEMENT VS NO GUARANTEE MUST PERSUADE MEDIA

When you buy ad space, it gives you a guarantee that the ad would be displayed at the given place. However, when you pursue a PR strategy, there is no guarantee that your communication would be displayed in the media channels. The media will cover your story only if they are convinced that it will be of interest to their readers. Thus, advertisement is guaranteed placement whereas PR does not give any guarantee.

CONTROL OVER FINAL PRINTS VS NO CONTROL

As we already saw earlier, in an ad you have the final control over what will be displayed. At the same time, you do not have any control over what will be displayed in the final version of a press release. You come up with a release but then how it is interpreted by the media and what words they select to write down the message is not in your hand. It is in the hands of the journalists. Thus, a series of such uncontrolled letters will determine how people feel when they look at you.

ADS ARE MOSTLY VISUAL VS PR IS TEXTUAL OR VERBAL

Ads are generally more visual than PR. In ads, you can use aesthetics and designs to deliver the message. Now, you need to understand that people subscribe to/buy magazines, newspapers, blogs, or other mediums for their content which includes news coverage, informative articles, and so on. People watch TV channels and other video streaming apps for their content and not for ads. Since the media houses focus on getting good content on their platform, the PR coverage tends to be articulated in a formal manner.

On the other hand, if you buy ad space on these, your ad needs to be stand out, and hence they are designed creatively and are visually attractive. If ads do not appeal to them, viewers/users do not complain. But if the content is not interesting, they would give up on the media channel. That is why ads are delivered creatively while the PR coverage is formal and textual in nature.

So these are the major differences between an ad and a Public relation effort. We now know what is a Public Relation campaign and what is an ad campaign. In understanding the difference from an ad campaign, we also understood the important features of a PR campaign. We know that it is relatively much cheaper, reach is not guaranteed, the final words of the article are not in our control, PR strategy might not interest the journalist at all, and so on.

Keeping all these in mind, let us proceed to understand more about Public relations and how powerful an underutilized method of marketing is.

CHAPTER THREE

WHO SHOULD HAVE A PR STRATEGY

Now that we know what is PR and what it can do, we need to understand who should use a Public Relations strategy? A PR strategy is relatively efficient in terms of cost but is expensive in terms of effort and time.

Having a PR strategy in place will demand a good amount of your time and resources. So the question that arises – Should every business owner invest this time and efforts in a PR strategy?

Before we answer the above question, let us understand the perspective of a media house owner or a journalist who covers such stories. For once, let us swap places. Let us say, you are a journalist. The magazine that you work for has a reader base that is interested in new entrepreneurial stories and successes and how different people got there.

The readership is majorly inclined towards interesting startups. Now because you are a journalist, you receive a few hundred press releases every week and you have to decide which stories you wish to cover and which stories you do not wish to cover.

Let us say someone sent you a story where a 30-year-old man started a textile business. In another announcement, another 30-year-old man started a company that aims to make flying cars. Another man started a company that directly challenges Flipkart and Amazon in India. Success or not is secondary, but whom do you think will the journalist more likely cover? The man starting a textile firm would not be his priority. He would most likely talk about a man starting a company about flying cars. Right?

Why would the journalist cover that story and not the textile one? The reason is simple and clear. The company trying to create flying cars is doing something new. The company trying to take on Amazon and Flipkart is doing something different.

After all, how many aim to take on Amazon and Flipkart. But the person starting the textile firm, is he doing something new? No. Is he doing something different? No. Thus, the chances that you as a journalist will cover him is very low. Now let us add some more facts. After starting the textile business, within 3 years he crossed the revenue benchmark of Rs. 100 crores.

After 5 years, his team was able to come up with an innovation using which the entire industry could increase their production by 2x in the same resources. Now would you cover him as a journalist? Is he doing something new? Is he doing something different? The answer most likely is, yes

Why would you do this? This is because of the audience. If something is new or different or both, only then will the audience be interested. Thus, even as a journalist, you can only cover stories that will actually interest the audience of your publication.

So, coming back to the question - "Who should have a PR strategy and put in the time and effort required by the same?" Well, the answer is – everyone should have it a little bit but only a few should have PR at the center of their marketing strategy. But only a few should depend on it with PR being at the center of their marketing plan.

WHO SHOULD HAVE PR AT THE CENTRE OF THEIR MARKETING PLAN

We saw that only a few should have PR at the center of their marketing strategy. The question is – Who all should? The answer to this is - those who have elements of 'new' or 'different' or both to their business.

If what you are doing is new or different or both or any component of your business model is new or different and would interest the audience, you can have a PR strategy. This is a subjective decision that every business owner must make.

We have included a list of items that can interest an audience. If your answers to those questions are new or different, then you would want to put in the PR efforts in getting them noticed

Go through the list and decide whether you are doing new

and different or not. If yes, go ahead. However, not all PR will get you sales. Some may only build recognition for your company and not get you direct sales immediately.

For now, know that anything that has a chance of being covered should be communicated to the media outlets in order to add credibility to your name. Particularly, if you are a small business.

Thus, only those that have anything 'New' or 'Different' or both shall have PR at the center of their marketing plan. If you are carrying out operations just the way others are, having a PR plan at the center of marketing will not get you the results that you want.

However, having said that, all businesses should do some basic PR management. Something is different about each and they should try and get creditability to their name by PR.

IS IT ONLY FOR THE BIG

A common misunderstanding amongst people is that they think PR is only for the big companies and that is why small business owners get intimidated and never put together a PR plan. However, the truth is the opposite. Journalists are looking for businesses of all sizes to interest their audience. In fact, people love David and the Goliath stories. The audience also loves rags to riches stories. The audience loves to know about struggles as they can then relate with the same.

Thus, the answer to the question – No, PR is not just for the big. It is for everyone who is doing anything that is new or different. If you think you are on this path, go ahead and set up a PR strategy in place.

The channels can be various. By channel, we mean that platform where your story is featured. It can be a newspaper, a magazine, an appearance in a podcast series, TV shows, news channels, blogs, and so on. This is an endless list. In fact, those who are big only require large channels to make a difference for them.

However, those that are small have multiple small channels available for them too. For instance, getting covered by a blog that has a few thousand subscribers might not change fortunes for a large company, but can definitely do so for a small company. Influencers can also help the companies.

Thus, by no means should the small companies think that PR is only for the larger players. PR can do for a small company what advertisement can never do. PR is one of the most powerful sources to earn creditability for a small business.

13th Mar 2020

This entrepreneur's approach to B2B ecommerce earns his procurement platform Rs 2.5 Cr per month

STORIES

18th Dec 2019

How a bus driver's son quit college and started a Rs 1 Cr turnover coworking space booking platform

STORIES

3rd Jan 2020

These MBA graduates quit their jobs to build a Rs 7.9 Cr B2B marketplace for granite exports

STORIES

19th Oct 2019

How these young Bengaluru founders started up in a basement and took their business to Rs 3 Cr revenue

STORIES

CHAPTER FOUR

WRITE A PRESS RELEASE

Here are some items about which you can write a press release. These are events that may interest a journalist. These are topics that are different from ordinary business and do not happen every day. These should get the required attention by the media outlets.

However, know that not all of it would be covered. But if you consistently keep the media outlets posted, then they should cover some of it and hence get you the desired attention. So, these events include-

1. A NEW PRODUCT LAUNCH
2. AN OLD PRODUCT WITH A NEW NAME OR PACKAGE
3. A PRODUCT IMPROVEMENT
4. A NEW VERSION OR MODEL OF AN OLD PRODUCT
5. AN OLD PRODUCT AVAILABLE IN NEW MATERIALS, COLORS, OR SIZES.
6. A NEW APPLICATION OF AN OLD PRODUCT.
7. NEW ACCESSORIES AVAILABLE FOR AN OLD PRODUCT.

8. THE PUBLICATION OF NEW OR REVISED SALES LITERATURE - BROCHURES, CATALOGUES, DATASHEETS, SURVEYS, REPORTS, REPRINTS, BOOKLETS ETC.
9. A SPEECH OR PRESENTATION GIVEN BY AN EXECUTIVE.
10. A CONTROVERSIAL ISSUE
11. NEW EMPLOYEES
12. PROMOTIONS WITHIN THE FIRM
13. AWARDS AND HONORS WON BY YOUR FIRM OR ITS EMPLOYEES
14. ORIGINAL DISCOVERIES OR INNOVATIONS
15. NEW STORES, BRANCHES, HEADQUARTERS, FACILITIES ETC.
16. NEW SALES REPS, DISTRIBUTORS, AGENTS.
17. MAJOR CONTRACTS AWARDED TO YOUR FIRM.
18. JOINT VENTURES
19. MANAGEMENT REORGANIZATION
20. MAJOR ACHIEVEMENTS SUCH AS UNITS SOLD, QUARTERLY EARNINGS, SAFETY RECORD ETC
21. UNUSUAL PEOPLE, PRODUCTS OR WAYS OF DOING BUSINESS
22. CASE HISTORIES OF SUCCESSFUL APPLICATIONS, INSTALLATIONS AND PROJECTS
23. TIPS AND HINTS
24. CHANGE IN COMPANY NAME, SLOGAN OR LOGO
25. OPENING OF A NEW BUSINESS
26. CHARITABLE ACTS
27. SPECIAL EVENTS SUCH AS A SALE, PARTY, OPEN HOUSE, PLANT TOUR, CONTEST, OR SWEEPSTAKES

CHAPTER FIVE

WHY PR

REACH VS COST

Press coverage in a newspaper gives the same reach as an ad in the same newspaper at a very low cost. You would be charged for the ads based on the viewership but the same is free if earned through PR. So, PR gives you a better reach at a lower cost than Advertisements.

TRUST

Imagine Times Of India showing your ad and the same newspaper writing an article about you? What is more trustworthy? The article right? The reason is that you have paid the newspaper to show your ad. But, you have not given them anything to write an article about you. The audience knows this and thus they understand that the article is honestly written.

ZERO BUDGET MARKETING

CHAPTER SIX

HOW PR & ADVERTISING GO TOGETHER

1. PR BUILDS CREDIBILITY AND THEN ADVERTISING SPREADS IT

Particularly for startups, if PR and ads are used together appropriately, they can do wonders. For this, first, you need put in the efforts to earn some credibility through PR. Once you have an adequate amount of credibility, use advertising to reach more people. When people respond to your ads, show them your PR coverage to earn their trust and make a sale to them.

In this way, you get an adequate reach and you earn their trust. If only one of them is used, you either get a good reach with limited credibility, or you earn trust but lack reach. Thus, use your resources

2. PR WILL TAKE TIME

We have already seen that nothing is promised with our PR efforts. Also, it takes time to shape a person's thinking about a particular subject. Thus, know that PR will take time. Many young entrepreneurs are in such haste that they skip this due to their impatience and move directly to the advertisement and thus do not get the required results. It is very important to keep in mind, PR will take time.

3. CONSERVE AD RESOURCES TILL CREDIBILITY IS EARNED

In the previous ebook 'Ads that Sell', we discussed that the ball is in your court till the time you have not spent your advertising budget. Thus, whenever marketing, you need to conserve your resources untill enough credibility is earned.

Once you are in a position to get people to trust you, only then shall you move ahead with spending your advertisement budget. Till then conserve your resources.

4. PR CREATES A BRAND, ADVERTISEMENT SUPPORTS IT

The truth is that all brands are created by the attention it receives. Only if the attention is trustworthy, will they be able to get the desired results. Thus, know that PR efforts are required for people to trust a brand. A popular brand can be created only through PR. Advertising can later be used to defend the position of the brand. To remind the people that the brand is about this particular subject.

For instance, when Amazon started, they needed PR to create a brand image in the minds of the people. Only after the trust had been earned, they could use advertisements to remind people that they should buy from Amazon. They did not have to do the difficult task of winning the trust through ads. Thus, we can say - PR creates a brand whereas advertisement defends it.

5. IMPOSSIBLE TO CREATE SOMETHING USING ONLY AN ADVERTISEMENT

It is impossible to create something only via advertising. The reason for that is ads facilitate only one-way communication. The reader reads whatever you have to say. Thus, he may not trust you blindly. And once you reduce your advertisement budget, chances are that he will forget you. This is because you do not stand for anything in his mind.

He remembers you only till the time you remind him of your presence. However, with PR this is not the case. You take a particular place in his mind. That is why we say, it is impossible to create something using only ads.

The bottom line is clear. First, get credibility using PR. It will take time. And only after that shall you use advertisement budget to reach more and more people.

CHAPTER SEVEN

CREATING A PR STRATEGY

Now that we know about Public relations – about its basics, how they are effective, how to use them, it is very important to put a PR strategy in place. A strategy that is systematic and makes sure that over a period of time you get the results that you need.

If you do not have a defined strategy in place, it becomes very difficult to achieve the desired results. This is because sending out any random release may not necessarily get you covered. You get covered only when you send out a series of coordinated and well-directed sets of messages to different media houses.

Here, we will learn about creating a PR strategy for our business. This PR template can be used by businesses, organizations, or even individuals to manage their public relations. We will create a strategy keeping all this in mind to maximize our PR campaign's effectiveness. Follow the steps discussed going forward to form a PR campaign for your business.

1. *IDENTIFY YOUR TARGET AUDIENCE*

2. *CREATE A STRATEGY FOR EACH TARGET AUDIENCE*

3. *CONTACT MANAGEMENT TO EXECUTE THE STRATEGY*

4. *COPYWRITE THE PRESS RELEASE TO GET IT COVERED*

CHAPTER EIGHT

STEP 1 - IDENTIFY TARGET AUDIENCE

The very first step is to identify the target audience. Which relations do you want to focus on using a PR strategy? Having discussed PR till now, many might think that a firm only needs to maintain PR with its target customers. That is as far from the truth. Businesses have various relations with different stakeholders. Each relation has different importance.

Thus, the firms have to decide based on their time and resources available as to which relation they want to focus on.

 **PUBLIC**
Opinion formers, Media, Online Communities

 **FINANCIAL**
Financial online and offline media, Shareholders/ owners and banks

 **INTERNAL**
Employees, Management/ directors, Potential staff

 **COMMERCIAL**
Suppliers, wholesalers/retailers, Potential customers

 **GOVERNMENT**
Parliamentarians, Civil Service, Local Government

 **OVERSEAS**
Customers, Governments, Business Partners

This is an exhaustive list of different types of relations that a business has. It is not mandatory that a business has all these relations but those that it has can be categorized in one of these categories and then sub-categories.

Now, you know the different stakeholders in your business and each relation serves a different purpose. Your relation with banks and investors is to meet your financing needs whereas your firm's relations with the internal team is to maintain the internal environment and the morale of employees and the team.

Also, each relation varies in priority based on the nature of the business. For instance, for a business that requires a lot of permissions and licenses, a relationship with the government would be very high in priority whereas a business that is in the service industry would have to focus a lot on internal relations. Businesses that have high capital requirements need to focus on Financial relations whereas export businesses need to focus on Overseas relations.

Businesses often need to focus on a bunch of these relations that they want to manage activities and the rest can be managed passively. This is where PR comes into the picture. The relations that have to be managed actively need to have a Public Relations Strategy. You need to communicate with them in a manner that your business's purpose is met.

The number of relations that can be chosen depends on the resources that a firm has. A large corporate actively manages all the relations that they may have because they can invest adequate time and resources. However, for a small firm, a bare minimum includes managing customer relations, employee relations, and public relations.

A small firm must actively invest time and energy in managing at least these relations. Other than that, they can decide if any other relation is high on priority based on the nature of their business. Maintaining employee relations is more related to your HR activities. Here in marketing, we will focus on customer and public relations management through PR that impacts your sales directly.

Not all relations are related to marketing directly, yet the method discussed going forward can be used to manage any relation in the audience.

CHAPTER NINE

STEP 2 - CREATING A PLAN FOR EACH AUDIENCE

Once we have identified our target audience with whom we wish to manage an active public Relation, keeping in mind the resources that we have, next we need to design a strategy for each of these audience groups. We need to have a strategy for each target audience and carry them out separately.

Here are the questions that we need to answer to make a strategy for each of the target audience groups. This list was first introduced by Joanne Barnett in 2006. This is still one of the most powerful methods to write a PR strategy. Answer these questions for each target audience and you will have a strategy ready to execute.

1. WHERE ARE WE NOW IN TERMS OF QUALITY OF RELATION?
2. WHERE DO WE WANT TO BE?
3. TO WHOM ARE WE TALKING ABOUT?

4. WHAT DO WE WANT THEM TO DO AND WHY DO WE WANT THEM TO DO IT?
5. WHAT ARE WE GOING TO SAY TO THEM (THE MESSAGE)?
6. WHERE ARE WE GOING TO REACH THEM?
7. WHEN ARE WE GOING TO REACH THEM?
8. WHICH TECHNIQUES OR METHODS ARE WE GOING TO USE TO REACH THEM?
9. HOW MUCH ARE WE GOING TO SPEND?
10. HOW DID WE DO?

So, let us say we have selected three audience sets that we want to manage PR with. These are – Suppliers, customers, and media. So in order to form a strategy, we will need to answer the above set of questions thrice – once for each set. It is pretty much the same as forming the one-page marketing plan for each customer segment we had identified.

Now that you know what is to be done, let us move forward and understand all these questions one by one.

WHERE ARE YOU NOW IN TERMS OF QUALITY OF RELATION?

The very first step of forming a PR plan is to understand the kind of relationship you have currently. Let us say, you are trying to manage relations with the general public using media, you need to understand what the public and media currently feel about you. It can be negative as well as positive. At times, there might be so many good stories floating about you that people are more receptive whenever you try and say something.

At other times, people may hold negative opinions about you and therefore might be unwilling to welcome anything positive about you. The media might also be unwilling to write about you. Thus, the very first step is to know what is the current quality of relation. Also, you need to be specific here. If people think negatively about you – what are the possible reasons why they think negatively about you? Be as specific as possible.

WHERE DO WE WANT TO BE?

The next step is to understand what your goals are with the PR effort, what do you want them to change in terms of how they think about you, what do you want them to think about you, and so on. Here again, be as specific as possible. Once you know what you want them to think about you, you select the messages accordingly. To be clear, what do you want them to think about you!

TO WHOM ARE YOU TALKING TO?

We already know the target audience. Here, the actual task is to research the target audience. For instance, if you are writing to the media, you need to understand what motivates them to take the action that you desire. If you are talking to a particular department in the Government, you need to understand the working of that department and what are the points that get them to take the action that you want. Thus, it is very important to know about the one you are talking to.

WHAT DO YOU WANT THEM TO DO AND WHY DO YOU WANT THEM TO DO IT?

You want your relationship to be in a certain manner with the target audience. This, however, would not be for no reason. Your business is a reason as to why you want the target to think about you in a certain way. Here, you need to clearly identify what are your business motives out of the relation. What exact actions do you want them to take – whether write good about you in the newspapers so that your creditability increases, get licenses with ease, ensure regular supplies, etc.

And also, you need to identify why do you want them to take those actions? It gives clarity to anyone or in fact even yourself when you are following up on the PR plan.

WHAT ARE YOU GOING TO SAY?

Now, this is the most important part. In a PR campaign, it is all about what you say that makes or breaks the campaign. If it interests the person, then the campaign would be effective. Else, it would not be that effective. We have already discussed the ideas earlier about what to say with a list.

The bottom line is, whatever you say should either be 'New' or 'Different' or both. Keep in mind that it is not possible to have a complete list of messages at the planning stage itself. As business goes on and new events take place, you get new messages that should be delivered. PR is a continuous activity.

WHERE ARE YOU GOING TO REACH THEM?

The next question deals with the medium that you are going to use to reach the target audience. For instance, you may know a few journalists personally. For them, you can talk to them via simple mail. However, to know more journalists, you might attend fairs, events or even drop a cold email asking them to meet in person. There is no right answer for what will work. But if you keep trying, over time, you will know enough people to make a difference.

You can do this for each target audience that you have identified. For instance, you will have to ask for appointments to manage PR with government officials, give interviews to media professionals, write letters to staff, and so on.

WHEN ARE YOU GOING TO REACH THEM?

If in your industry, there are certain times in the year, when people are more likely to hear what you are doing and cover the story, you should target those months of the year. For instance, some industries are free just after the end of the financial year as the workload goes down. Some are occupied just after the financial year ends. Some Industries have a peak workload during the festival season. So, you need to understand, when are you reaching out to people.

Also, another important thing is that you need to keep in mind the timeline of your activities. For instance, if you have a major product launch coming up, you need to plan and time PR activities such that you get the maximum benefit out of these.

WHICH TECHNIQUES ARE YOU GOING TO USE?

There are a few techniques that firms use for PR management. These are listed on the following pages. You can use these tools to manage PR and get the required attention. You can also come up with your own tricks and methods to get the attention of your target audience. Some basic techniques include – writing a press release, sponsoring or hosting events, giving speeches, etc.

All these would be discussed going forward. Be selective about the techniques to be used keeping in mind the behavior of the target audience.

HOW MUCH ARE YOU GOING TO SPEND?

There are a few techniques that firms use for PR management. These are listed on the following pages. You can use these tools to manage PR and get the required attention. You can also come up with your own tricks and methods to get the attention of your target audience. Some basic techniques include – writing a press release, sponsoring or hosting events, giving speeches, etc.

All these would be discussed going forward. Be selective about the techniques to be used keeping in mind the behavior of the target audience.

HOW DID YOU DO?

The very last step is feedback. Based on the feedback you need to make changes in your PR strategy. Honest feedback and review play a very important part in improving your PR strategy. However, a common problem is many beginners review their PR strategy after every message or every month. Do not do so. PR takes time to bear results.

Do not review your strategy with a gap of fewer than 3 months. That is the bare minimum that PR takes to have results. That too only if you are a small business. For larger companies, they should not review their PR strategy with a gap of fewer than 6 months. Thus, keep in mind, the review is an important step in PR activities but an adequate gap is important in reviews.

Thus, these are the questions that shall be answered to form a strategy for any given target audience. If you do it for all the selected target audiences, you will have an effective PR plan in place about how you want to manage different relations that your business has. As you gain more resources, you can start managing more relations actively. Remember, a good relationship always reduces friction in the business.

CHAPTER TEN

STEP 3 - CONTACT MANAGEMENT

Now that you have a PR strategy in place, you need a list of contacts to whom you will be sending your communication. For instance, if you are going to maintain a PR with suppliers, who exactly in the Supplier firm will you contact. Also, given a large number of supplier firms, you will have a set of contact persons that need to be communicated with the same set of information.

Similarly, when releasing a Press Release, you need a list of journalists, who work with different media houses who will take your message forward and will cover it in their publication. Thus, the third important step to be taken is contact management. Having a list of contacts who you will approach with your messages.

The list is not just any random list. It is put together very carefully to include as many people as possible who are likely to cover your story. Creating that list is an ongoing effort and takes time and effort. You will keep adding names as you go along with your PR plan. You need to take the steps to find out journalists who cover the topics that you are working on.

For instance, if you are in the automobile sector, you need journalists who talk about this particular sector. Only then your chances of being covered will go up.

On the next page, we have given a template that should be filled to maintain a list of contacts. One is for maintaining PR with various media outlets whereas the second will be handy when you try and maintain a relationship with any other industry. Keep filling these templates for each target audience and you will have a series of contacts ready. Have as many quality contacts as possible. But do not fill the template with low-quality leads that have a very narrow chance of covering you and your story.

CONTACT MANAGEMENT FOR MEDIA

OUTLET	COVERAGE AREA	EDITOR	CONTACT

CONTACT MANAGEMENT FOR FIRMS

FIRM	RELATION TO BUSSINESS	MANAGER	CONTACT

INDIVIDUAL CONTACT MANAGER

Lastly, when you have made a list of all contacts to whom you would be sending each piece of communication, you also need an individual contact with more details about the key person to be contacted. Why this? The reason is pretty simple. You need to know the contact person at a personal level as well. It is very important to be well researched about him.

You need to fill out an individual contact management template like the one shown on the next page. It has all the details about individuals that you need to know to communicate properly with him. In the following template, 'About' is a very important row. You need to write about the contact person, their education, work background, stand on important matters in the industry, opinions about certain topics that they might have expressed in public, etc.

They allow you to know the person much better and then when writing a Press release or any other form of communication, you can use these facts about them to your advantage to increase your chances of being covered.

If you write something they already believe in, the chances of them mentioning and covering your story go up significantly. Thus, do the research. This is your edge. Do the research about your key contact persons. In this manner, you need to manage your contacts. First, you will need a list of all the key contact persons and then you will need information about them individually too. This is one of the most important steps to execute your PR strategy.

Once you have a contact list, the next step is just to send them the correct messages.

INDIVIDUAL CONTACT MANAGEMENT

NAME	
COMPANY	
POSITION	
EMAIL	
PHONE	
SOCIAL MEDIA	
ABOUT	

CHAPTER ELEVEN

STEP 4 – WRITING PR COMMUNICATION

Now, we will see a few points that you need to keep in mind when writing a public relation communication piece. You can use these principles to write a press release as well. These principles apply to all kinds of PR messages irrespective of the target audience.

You need to use these whether writing to your suppliers, customers, government officials, members of the press, etc. These are very important pieces of communication and shall determine your relations going forward.

DO NOT SELL

The very first thing you need to keep in mind when writing a PR communication is that you should not sell. Any message that focuses on selling makes the receiver feel that the writer is not interested in the relationship but in the outcome only. This feeling of the receiver will reduce the effectiveness of your PR campaign.

Thus, the first thing to keep in mind is – Do not sell. Be soft and just put across your point. If the receiver is interested, he will follow up.

WRITE FOR THE AUDIENCE

When writing a PR communication, you will be sending it to a contact person, whether it be in a firm, in a government, or in the press. But you do not want them to keep the message to themselves. You want them to spread the message to your intended audience.

In a firm, they must take the message to their seniors, in a government body the message must reach the position holders and authorities and when writing to the press the message must be covered in the newspaper to reach the public. Thus, whenever writing a PR communication, make sure to write it keeping the end audience in mind i.e. what shall get them interested.

SUBJECT LINE IS VERY CRITICAL

Whenever writing a PR communication, your message would be judged by the subject line of the mail or the letter. That will decide if the reader opens your letter or not. Thus, keep in mind that you sum up the entire story in the subject line. It can be up to two lines here. Use the methods of writing headlines discussed in the copywriting ebook 'The Journal of Copywriting'.

GET STRAIGHT TO THE POINT

When you begin the body, do not waste time talking about irrelevant topics. Get straight to the point as soon as possible. The lead will decide if the person reads the entire message or not. If the lead is weak, the reader would not continue reading.

At the lead stage itself, make sure you give him the details of the message that you are trying to convey - who, when, where, what and how. Do not leave him looking for answers in the main body about the event. The following body of the message can be used for more details.

USE THE BODY FOR ADDITIONAL FACTS

Once you have explained the event in the lead paragraph, only those who are interested will continue to read the full body. So, when you are writing the body, you can assume that the person has some degree of interest in your story.

Now, use the body to elaborate the story with additional facts and details. Be as specific as possible. Use evidence to support whatever you are saying. Use quotes, testimonials, and images to show proof of whatever you are saying. Use the body to build credibility to your story.

DO NOT USE FLOWERY LANGUAGE, JARGONS AND HYPE

Just like writing any other piece of marketing communication, this principle applies to writing a PR communication as well. Do not use fancy flowery language in your communication that overshadows the message. Use simple language so that the message can be clearly understood and the focus does not shift from message to the language.

Next, avoid using jargon so that the message can be clearly understood. Once the message starts using jargon, the listener often goes into a shell because of the effort it will require. Lastly, do not create hype as well. No one likes hype. The moment a person feels hype, he becomes less attentive to the message. Thus, whenever writing any PR communication, make sure to keep these in mind.

STICK TO FACTS

PR is to build creditability. To do so, you cannot have a message full of opinions and no facts. A journalist or in fact any other person will not push the message forward if it lacks in substance and only has language and opinions. Thus, whenever writing PR, make sure you give them substance. Make sure you stick to facts.

GIVE THEM SOMETHING MENTIONING

Many communicators fall into a trap and in order to maintain the frequency of their communication, they end up writing PR messages that have no substance to them. Do not do this. It reduces the value of your message in the receiver's eyes.

Next time, even if you mention something very important, they might not be open to reading the entire text just because it is from you. Thus, make sure to give them something worth mentioning. Something that has a story.

LENGTH OF THE MESSAGE

Do not write PR messages that are too long. The ideal length of a PR message is less than one page but if you are talking about something very critical and important, you can go up to two pages. Do not write a PR message longer than 2 pages under any condition particularly when you are a startup and no one knows you. Keep the length of the message adequate.

CONTACT DETAILS

Next, before finishing a PR message, make sure to include a contact person's name and contact details so that the reader can reach out in case he needs more clarity. Do not give a corporate number with multiple extensions, give a particular person's specific number so that the reader can reach this person with ease.

Also, the contact person must be someone who is familiar with the details of the message and also is allowed to speak to the public or anyone outside the firm.

CORPORATE PROFILE

The very last thing to do is give a corporate profile in the end. Even if the person knows you and your company, it's better to give a corporate profile. The reader will find it easy to explain what you do exactly. Else, he would be left in the middle ground. Thus, make sure that you explain your business in the end. This should be around 100 words. No more than that.

These are the important things that you need to keep in mind when writing a PR message. This way you can carry out an effective PR campaign that significantly changes the relations you have with the outsiders. Keep it simple and follow these steps. Do not complicate the process.

CHAPTER TWELVE

TOOLS FOR PR

Lastly, these are the common tools used to maintain PR. You can use any of these to send out your message or you can think of new and creative tools. However, these are the tried and tested ones and if done with a proper strategy as discussed earlier, these tools can be very effectively utilized to get the kind of response you want from your PR campaign.

1. WRITE AND DISTRIBUTE PRESS RELEASES
2. SPEECH WRITING FOR BUSINESS TO BE GIVEN BY EXECUTIVES AT VARIOUS EVENTS
3. WRITE PITCH ABOUT THE BUSINESS AND SEND THEM DIRECTLY TO JOURNALISTS
4. ORGANIZE SPECIAL EVENTS DESIGNED FOR PUBLIC AND MEDIA RELATIONS
5. CONDUCT MARKET RESEARCH ON THE FIRM OR FIRM'S MESSAGING
6. PERSONAL NETWORKING OR ATTENDING / SPONSORING EVENTS
7. WRITING AND BLOGGING FOR THE WEB
8. CRISIS PUBLIC RELATIONS
9. RESPONSE TO NEGATIVE OPINIONS ONLINE

CHAPTER THIRTEEN

CONCLUSION

Now you know enough to create your PR campaign and start practicing PR. We have already discussed how it should be used. With this we end our discussion on Public Relation. Now you know you can work on any relation with a proper PR strategy in place. So, begin your practice.

www.ingramcontent.com/pod-product-compliance
Lightning Source LLC
Chambersburg PA
CBHW070837220526
45466CB00002B/810